A Bite-Sized I

My Other Car is an Aston

A Practical Guide to Ownership and Other Excuses to Quit Work and Start a Business

Stuart Haining ACIB, MCIM

Published by Bite-Sized Books Ltd 2018

Bite-Sized Books Ltd

ISBN: **9781982904609**

Published by:

Bite-Sized Books Ltd
Cleeve Croft, Cleeve Road, Goring RG8 9BJ UK
information@bite-sizedbooks.com
Registered in the UK. Company Registration No: 9395379

Author's Warning

I'm sorry, but anyone buying this book in the belief it might also be a *self-help, get-rich-quick* guide to starting a business should think again!

Yes, I do indeed waffle on a bit about how owning a company can get you the car, if not the girl, but it's mostly an unusual take on motoring, and in particular the unexpected joys and pitfalls of owning an Aston Martin for the first time.

Hopefully it's a light-hearted look at the kinds of things you won't find in any other car book on the planet either!

As always my thanks go out to my publishers for putting up with me and spotting things I don't have the skills in English to get right, or should that be write?!

Contents

Chapter 1

Introduction

For many people, the thought of emulating a James Bond lifestyle (more on that later!) means they have the desire to own an Aston Martin embedded from a very early age – I wasn't like that at all. I arrived in the unusual world of Aston Martin entirely by accident (and more about the accident later too!). It's true of course that I'm a bit of a car nut, and owning a snazzy car was always on my agenda however much I might have kept it a secret and denied it to her-who-shall-be-obeyed, Mrs H (That's Mrs H the wife, not Mrs H the mum). Each Mrs H would of course, being sensible, probably agree not to agree with me about cars, even if like most mothers/daughters-in-law they don't see eye-to-eye on much else!

In fact, I could go even further and admit that owning a snazzy car was even one of the main reasons for starting my own company a decade earlier, and I kept that a secret too as it's hardly the rationale you are expected to give for starting a business is it?

My thought was that starting a business would help get me a step closer to a **Maserati**, the GranTurismo coupe version if you know it? And have you seen that interior?

WOW.

And they say Italians are only any good at handbags and ladies shoes. Whoever *they* may be, they need to know that the Italians can certainly rival the British when it comes to cool car interiors crafted from the finest soft leathers!

Editor's Note

Isn't it odd that in addition to Italian cars you also like Italian handbags and Italian ladies' shoes! Is there something you're not telling us here?

Author

No, I do like them as well but don't buy them for wearing myself!

Anyway, back to the subject in hand, my desired Maserati. The outside of said vehicle isn't exactly an eye-sore either. So that was always my goal, get a black Maserati with a cream or red leather interior and I thought starting my own business was a good route to achieve the goal. So, let's take you on a journey (a shortish one, I promise) through to how I ended up in the exciting world of Aston Martin ownership instead of Maserati. I hope you enjoy the journey and learn a few unexpected things that certainly won't be covered in the run-of-the-mill car or business/money management books!

PS, there are indeed a few comments regarding excuses to start a business, but as I've admitted already, if it's business advice you need, this is probably not the right vehicle for you (get what I did there?), have a look at Professor Malcolm McDonald's excellent marketing books instead... I owe him a big favour for his kind review of my own business books and his suggestion that they are a little cheeky!)

Chapter 2

From Early Beginnings and Toy Cars

Of course, I always had toy cars as a boy and remember fondly having a silver Corgi 007 DB5, complete with red interior, (and this passion for red did survive my childhood – both my **Aston V8 Vantage**, my short journey car, and my **Alfa Romeo BreraS**, my longer journey car as it's diesel, might be considered as pimp-mobiles since both are complete with top to toe **red leather** interiors.)

Needless to say I hope they look more stylish in real-life than they do talking about it in print.

I think the love of leather goes back decades earlier to playing in my dad's warehouse – he was a leather-factor for the shoe trade. I used to mix the colours up and move the stock about to make a secret den, much to the annoyance of the poor employees who had to come in and re-organise things on a Monday morning. But the love of that leather smell persists to this day. I realise I'm lucky he didn't instead own a laundry specialising in dirty pants or other unmentionables, as that's much harder to replicate when it comes to buying a car!

Unlike the pristine packaging in the picture below (image courtesy of Corgi), the start of my love affair with nice cars wasn't destined to be lovingly preserved for posterity or collectors in boxes, (the toys in said boxes, not the collectors). My toy cars, including the DB5 which was pride of the fleet, were loved almost to destruction.

I'm almost like that to this day with my real cars too, believing they were envisaged, designed and manufactured to be enjoyed and driven, not preserved and hidden away in museums. So my cars, even the Aston Martin, are driven hard (within legal limits of course) and at some point the rev-limiter is sure to have kicked in with most if not all of them. And I get through brake pads quickly too which is probably more a commentary on my driving style than the cars' mechanical set-up or running costs.

My cars get used for trips to the local **refuse tip** and **DIY shops** (who else would fetch long fence posts in an Aston Martin, see below) and are used most days – this seems to be an unusual trait particularly amongst Aston owners. This is a shame as it means they are a relatively rare sight on the roads (Astons, not the owners –who I assume can get out just fine).

But I don't want you to get the wrong idea here – despite my vehicles being well used they are also well loved and well cared for, I try and keep them nice with a regular clean, and they get put away every night. The toys in a toy box, the real cars in an **alarmed** garage – not alarmed in the sense of being panicked at a sudden invasion of cars every night.

it's part of the house alarm system with sensors, the works.

Image courtesy Mrs H

Editor's Note

Am I mistaken or isn't that an extra bit of red leather on the underneath of the parcel shelf?

Author

I didn't like the black plastic and just happened to have a bit of red leather knocking around in almost the exact same shade – as most people no doubt do?

Chapter 3

Reasons to Start a Business?

Buying a nice car was one reason for starting my first business and I think in general it's always good to have a significant motivating factor to persuade yourself to take a big step like this. For me, the big step was leaving the relative well-paid security of working for a UK High Street Bank, into starting my own technology company.

I actually had three reasons to start a business.

- Firstly, it appealed to me to be able to create **jobs** for good people currently in less good jobs. I don't mean that in a patronising way as who's to say what's a good job and what isn't but we must all have seen people on our travels and thought *they're so much better than that job…..wish I could help them out?* Well, I decided I'd do more than wish it, I'd act. And my main goal was to build a company that could give good people a leg up in life…. assuming they were willing to work in marketing or IT of course, which isn't everyone's cup of tea for sure, but you can't have everything. (These are boring careers to some people, fun to others, personally I've always found that work, any work, breaks into my day terribly!)

- My second reason for starting a business, and probably the reason why you've acquired this little book (a big thanks by the way), and aside from the probably mistaken belief that starting a business is a guaranteed route to easy riches, was all about cars. In the Bank (I worked for two) they tended to have strange rules, sometimes these were unwritten policy, sometimes formal rules written in their short 600+ page staff handbook. I mean, honestly, who needs pages of staff rules like that?

Editor's Note

Your current staff manual in your own company is over 40 pages long, not forgetting a separate Risk and Health & Safety Manual!

Well in my early days in Banking, in the early 80's, it was an unwritten rule you couldn't buy a house in the same road as your boss – presumably due to some anarchic belief that this reinforced their hierarchy and power? It also extended to cars – you couldn't get a staff loan to buy a car better than your boss either, so if he or she had had a desire to buy say, a Yugo, you were proper screwed. Luckily not many did but it still wasn't a great policy, official or otherwise.

Anyone that knows me well will tell you I don't take such rules lying down – in fact it's like a red rag to a bull. Even if I hadn't been interested in cars I'd have been interested in seeking out this crazy rule and trying to break it. I did in fact do just this some years later at Barclaycard, managing to get a company paid-for Freelander when that was first launched, and strictly speaking it was above my pay grade! I achieved the seemingly impossible by picking a model one grade above my entitlement and then experimented on the price impact if I stripped out one factory fitted option at a time, until I hopefully hit my price point.

So I got a new Land Rover, when really I was only supposed to be able to order a Rover, as by de-specking that car it was now £100 into my price band. Obviously it's a little unusual to strip things out of a car's specification and boy did everyone get miffed when I turned up in the car park in my new car – they all assumed I'd been promoted when in fact I just had a 50%/50% rear seat instead of a 60%/40% version of managers one grade higher!

So you could probably say the longing for a nice car had the early seeds of desire planted 50 years ago by James Bond model cars and this was reinforced a decade or so later by the Bank's silly rules.

It was also building on a family tradition of enjoying nice cars – my grandad owned a 3-wheel Morgan so was pretty dashing in his day, and my dad owned several Jaguars with very smart interiors, and my half-brother had Jaguars and a Lotus, so it was probably inevitable I'd like cars someday too.

Image source Creative Commons

The final part of the jigsaw came in later years when I discovered that even if you *were* fortunate enough that the Bank did award you a company paid-for car with enough cash to get a decent model, they had different rules that would *still* stop you getting the **marque** you wanted, even if it cost no more. It begs the question *who thinks up these policies?*

Editor's Note

Didn't you write your own 40+ page manual?

So even if you were a Director, which I wasn't, with a huge allowance, which I didn't have, you still couldn't get a car like a Maserati or an Aston Martin, however much you cried, moaned or schemed.

Now, I'm sorry to say this, but however many extras it has I just don't consider a top of the range Nissan QX V6 SEL – an example from the time – as luxury in the same way, even if someone else is paying for it and it has every conceivable electrical gizmo you could ever want! (I do remember a Bank Director getting one of these beauties and probably paying about £35,000 which was a year's salary at the time so a lot of money!)

Image courtesy YouTube / Drive To Write

The message seemed clear to me – If you want a properly posh car you need to get on, get out, and start your own business. So I did, not forgetting of course that if you can succeed in your own business it's also a route to riches and maybe having a bit more control over your own and your family's destiny.

Editor's Note

You're intentionally glossing over the fact that if you earn enough you can of course buy your own car with your own hard-earned cash rather than getting your employer to buy it through their car scheme or leasing it for you! But I'll let it go for the simple reason that it's much more fun to have someone else pay for your car if possible!

So, I'm poised to quit the Bank and start my own business, partly in the hope of one day being able to create job opportunities for people and mostly in the hope of ending up with a nice car, and **wealth** probably being the third objective if I had to rank them. If putting cars higher up the agenda makes me vain, an egotist, or brand snob, so be it. I'm sorry, few people are perfect.

Author

In actual fact I cheated and I wasn't quite as brave as I've suggested.

I actually wangled a redundancy package to help fund my start-up business via a helpful boss, and the Bank let me keep the Land-Rover for 6 months, when I had simultaneously raised over £2m in venture capital to fund things.

So, whilst it's technically true that wanting a nice car was a part of my journey towards starting my own business, I was in fact risking other people's money more than my own even though it was of course still a risk giving up a good pay cheque and pension, but hopefully you get the general theme.

PS. Mrs H (wife) obviously never mentions that I gave up a well-paid job, except in arguments, so it's not an entirely risk-free strategy even with other people's money!

Anyway, hopefully you get the idea – if you want a car like an Aston Martin you probably need to man-up (or woman-up if that's even a phrase), take some risks, and do something like start your own business. I will go on to explain some other surprising ways of possibly achieving the same car ownership goal in a minute.

Chapter 4

The Goal Board

Now that I've mentioned the word Goal on a few occasions, if I had the time and space I should probably talk you through how the concept of a Goal Board really can help. I'd tell you that once I'd got my company started, the next task was create a mini-Goal Board and display it prominently next to my desk so I could be regularly exposed to images I'd added of reasons for starting my business, and things I'd wanted to achieve or purchase.

I'd read somewhere that once you visualise your goals and write them down you have something like an 800% greater chance of success, so that's what I did.

It was a strange board, pictures of cars, people in forgettable jobs, unforgettable supermodels, with a few pictures of things like a Hi-Fi and Italian Espresso Machine thrown in for good measure!

And I'd tell you that it does work, well almost! I'm still no nearer to any supermodels (but as I type this I am coincidentally off for a meeting with a celebrity) or owning a proper Espresso machine, but obviously I did get the posh car, hence this book. I'd be able to tell you that within just **3 years** of creating my Goal Board, complete with picture of a Maserati GranTurismo with me in the driving seat (not courtesy of very rude staff at Maserati Nottingham who actually refused to let me take a picture in the showroom so I had to sneak in during a trade show for a photograph and they'd luckily left the car unlocked!), I was eventually the lucky and proud owner of a true luxury car.

Not the most expensive in the world, but to me certainly one of the nicest as it was top-spec and like new.

But I haven't got time to tell you all that so I'll just say that having a Goal Board seemed like it may have been part of the reason for my success, albeit it was out on direction – it got the brand wrong and I ended my *journey* as the proud owner of a **pre-loved** Aston Martin Vantage, not a Maserati at all.

What is perhaps even more surprising is that I'd achieved my goal for little more than I might have spent on the aforementioned top-spec Nissan Maxima / QX had I not been such a brand snob.

Editor's Note

Now is probably a good time to mention that a Goal Board isn't ideal for everything, for example, if you'd been an astronaut targeting the Space Station (not the latest crashed one) it's not overly helpful to miss by a few miles and end up on Mars?

Anyway, just look at the difference between the cars (my own Aston is pretty similar to these pictures, a dark purple-black).

You might be able to see that in the earlier fence post picture, and the interior is of course red leather and red velvet-like woollen carpet. It's a tad nicer than the Nissan?

Images AM/ExeSport

Chapter 5

Affordability and Roseanne

I suppose before I go onto explain about how I stumbled willingly from Maserati to Aston Martin I should say a bit more about whether we could afford the car or not and what made us buy used instead of new? At the time of acquiring my Aston Martin we had circa enough family assets to purchase maybe 3 new Astons, but in reality, this supposedly *spare* cash was needed to fund a future pension. So we'd done OK out of life, in part because I am a very good manager of money – some would say mean! But I didn't buy new. I'd say that's as I'm just **careful**.

Editor's Note

Mean. You made me get – and pay for – the coffees!

To my mind it takes a long time to save cash, as you know, or a long time to build even a moderately successful business (at least for most people, including me) so I was not planning on parting with our money a whole lot quicker than we'd earned it. So whilst in theory we could afford new, I think generally it's good money management to have a rainy day fund on one side – so I started looking at older cars and luckily with luxury vehicles they generally have lower mileages anyway.

And aside from this common sense approach, why anyone would possibly want to buy three new Astons even if they could afford them?

I know some people do, but you can only drive one at a time! So a used car was our destiny due in part to the fact I'd messed up my pensions a bit earlier in life by opting out of a final salary (defined benefits) pension scheme two decades earlier and we had some catching up to do.

Editor's Note

I thought you said you were good with money?!

The point I'm trying badly to explain here is that we certainly weren't destitute and had spare assets, but we weren't so well off as to waste money or take big financial risks so my entry into the luxury car market was via second hand (or as I prefer to call it, pre-loved) adverts in the classifieds. So as car buyers our profile is probably not so different to many people?

Whilst on the subject of *pre-loved*, it's obviously a sentiment that's well understood and even spoofed.

Have you seen that infamous glamour girl photo that's been tampered with and does the rounds every few years online and hence is one of the world's biggest spoof adverts, yet somehow still builds the cache of the brand, even if it's in a cheeky non p/c way! It might almost pass for genuine if it weren't for the lazy typo **pre-*owed*** instead of **pre-*owned*.**

I'm sure the model **Rosanne Jongenelen** won't mind the publicity too much, nor the resulting complaint to Aston Martin from a journalist at ***Viewspaper***, although we're not so sure what the Aston brand police must make of it!

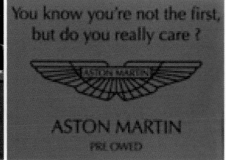

Nobody else bothers but we believe these Images are probably courtesy of Playboy Netherlands. We have included a second picture so you don't need to search for it yourself! Follow up image courtesy of Quora / The Viewspaper

We've subsequently learnt that contrary to what you might expect, any Aston Martin can still make a good investment, even under circumstances with tighter finances, versus say buying a newer but more ordinary new car for a similar budget. Pre-owned or pre-owed was therefore a good route for us, pun intended.

So my plan evolved to start looking for a good condition, nearly-new car which I planned to use on short journeys alongside my longer journey day car, my Alfa Romeo. I was aiming to get a car at around the MOT age, something circa 3 years old where depreciation had made it affordable and I set a budget of up to **£45,000**, so circa $50,000. And not so different to the price of a Nissan Maxima or whatever a similar model might be priced at today.

Editor and Author's Note

*We are not intentionally picking on Nissan, it's simply that at the relevant time in the story they wanted to enter the luxury market, and their Maxima models were indeed at comparable prices (new) to older cars from luxury brands, even though the latter often had lower specifications. We could make similar comparisons today with Toyota, Kia (see example below), Hyundai, Ford, Vauxhall, for example, who will all have premium priced models in their ranges. Depending on your point of view these might represent excellent value per gadget or on a profit margin basis but in my view are overpriced from a brand perspective, and this book is about **brands**.*

£45,000 is of course still a huge amount of money to most people, including me, not least because to truly afford it you've had to save that out of earned and taxed income after all other bills are paid, so you might need to realistically earn say £300,000 to have £45,000 *spare*.

I for one could not part with say £42,000 on a Kia Sorrento, see below. I'm sure just like the older Nissan QX of yesteryear it is indeed a lovely well-built car with loads of extras as standard, but if you are reading this book you'd probably agree it's hardly as exciting as an Aston Martin or Maserati.

So maybe that does indeed make the case that any hand-made car, even a pre-loved pre-owned one, is **great value**, provided it's reliable of course?

Image courtesy Kia

I had sold my business a couple of years prior to the purchase and was using part of the cash raised for the car, or that was the plan as I'd promised Mrs H (wife) that I wouldn't splash out on a so-called expensive car until we sold up. In practice, because of the aforementioned and alleged *mean* tendencies I still couldn't bring myself to part with the cash even when I had it. So I made my wife a new deal, based on *I wouldn't waste money on a car unless I made more money beyond my salary*, so that's what I set out to achieve and we advance sold our future business contracts for cash today – this paid for the car and my tax bills from the business sale! It was a win-win for all concerned. I got the kind of car I'd always dreamed of, Mrs H was happy as I hadn't gambled and taken huge risks, and the tax man got his money early too.

NB. If I'd realised a lovely Aston Martin, like mine, which was top-spec and I believe an original **Press Car**, could have been acquired for around a third of its original purchase price and yet still be, literally, as new (mine cost circa £115k new and was just **£41k** second-hand, after haggling, complete with warranty), I would have considered getting an Aston Martin many years earlier.

Chapter 6

Other Ways To Save

Now that we have a bit of a handle on the numbers involved I find it staggering to realise that almost anyone in any kind of job could theoretically at least save up for a pre-loved luxury car just by following a pre-thought through plan or one of the following crazy ideas, or in reality, a combination to maybe make it happen even quicker, perhaps even alongside starting a business:

- Give up that daily glass of wine at the pub. Time to save for an Aston Martin = 20 years,

- Stop that 10 a day cigarette habit when you're 20, own an Aston at your 40th birthday, and hopefully you'll live longer too. It'll take a bit longer if you give up vaping!

- Stop having a daily quality newspaper. And 40 years later you've got an Aston on the drive ready for your retirement,

- That weekly flower arrangement from the florists, gone, if you want an Aston in 20 years and you can enjoy different fragrances every day then.

It seems to me proven then that achieving the impossible of owning a truly luxurious vehicle can happen by starting and selling a successful business or giving up on a few modest regular purchases that you might not even miss. And this is to save up the equivalent of say £40,000 at today's prices. In practice, getting a car like an Aston could be even easier as prices do go lower than £40,000, and the same applies for Maseratis, Bentleys and even the odd Ferrari or two.

Here are some fairly typical deal examples from real life Aston Martins on sale at the time of writing this section in March 2018:

- On eBay Motors, this vehicle might cost £29,000 but you could have struck lucky for **half** that if buyers were absent and the reserve wasn't sensible. It's similar to my car.

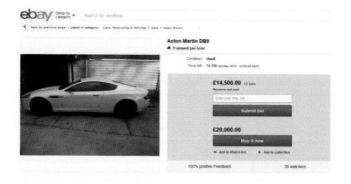

- And here's another, its only averaged around 5,000 miles per annum and one careful owner.

2006 Aston Martin Vantage 4.3 V8 2dr
65K+FSH+GREY/RED LEATHER+READ

£29,925.00
Classified Ad

Collection in person
Miles: 65,476
Brand: Aston Martin

- Or how about a DB9, even cheaper, and only 3,000 miles per annum for an 007 look-a-like.

Aston Martin DB9 2005 Low Mileage Immaculate Condition & Perfect Service History

The first owner was a man in his late 70's who had always wanted an Aston and treated himself to the car but only covered about 7,000 miles in the first 5 years. Aside from the above, the car has a perfect service history with 15 stamps in the book.

£26,200.00

8d 3h
Collection in person
Reg. Date: 2005
Miles: 41,700
Brand: Aston Martin

Ok, so we've established that pretty much anyone could afford a luxury car if they have the right habits, a bit of luck, start a business or simply saved up and shopped around. But how exactly did I go about finding my car?

Chapter 7

The Test Drive and Letraset

Luckily near us in Northamptonshire we have one of those **specialist car dealers** who sells every kind of luxury car imaginable from a giant B&Q sized **hangar** – so it's a veritable feast of Porsches, Astons, Bentleys, Maseratis, Range Rovers, Lamborghinis, Ferraris and the like, ranging in cost from around £20k to £350k for an occasional classic like a restored 007 style DB5. A quick look online confirmed they had my desired Maserati in stock, albeit with a cream interior not a red one. I booked a test drive – you need to book so they can check you out and prepare the car – this often means charging it up. The day of the test drive arrived and the car looked just like new, smelt like new, and it was a fantastic experience just to sit in the driving seat – properly this time with no sneaking around.

Off we went for a test drive on a new dual carriageway, so it was about as close to being at the Nurburgring or Silverstone (the latter not so many miles away as we live in the same county) as you could imagine, albeit with a speed limit and other cars to contend with! The test car was a petrol automatic, as so many of these luxury cars are, and I was made up (not literally, make-up isn't compulsory in a posh car, even if it is Italian!) at being one step nearer achieving something on my goal board.

Imagine then the absolute **horror** when I discovered to my surprise that the Maserati wasn't actually very nice to drive at all, despite a shared heritage with my Alfa Romeo. I'd go so far as to say it didn't even feel as nice as my older Brera, and that's a diesel for heaven's sake!

So I returned to the garage forlorn, and by that, I mean sad, not lonely (as the salesman was with me on the test drive!) and pronounced the car a stinker. I declared the Maserati wasn't for me after all, despite yearning for one for years, and prepared to leave. At this point the rather intuitive salesperson said, **well why not try this Aston V8 Vantage?** *It's a similar price and spec to the Maserati, but a rare manual gearbox*.

It was worth a shot even though I'd always considered Aston Martins a step up even beyond Maseratis and Ferraris. Surely they were expensive and being British they were probably more unreliable and hence costly to maintain? We all know 007 has a workshop of skilled technicians called Q, but I'd be dependent on local experts probably charging £350 an hour!

Anyway I decided let's be optimistic.

Externally the car was not so dissimilar to the Maserati. It was black for starters and a coupe. And it too had a super leather interior, this time in a rather snazzy tan leather with an evocative name that was something like **Red Fox**, so appropriate when you're test driving a car in a hunting county in the heart of the Midlands. This was when I learned that Astons aren't quite like an ordinary car, and by that, I mean probably not like *any* other car as they are very quirky.

- Firstly, when getting your driver briefing you notice that things like window switches are in fact **upside down** – presumably they'd salvaged parts from the Volvo or Jaguar parts bin (as former owners Ford also owned these marques) so if a desired part didn't fit, they'd make it fit, whichever way up it had to go!
- Then on to the hand-brake – I think to be factually correct I should say that on an Aston Martin they

typically fit a Racing Handbrake – but to me, it was a most odd thing. We all understand handbrakes, down equals off and up equals on, and they sit in the middle of the car? No, that's much too simple. In an Aston when its down it's on, or off (as it always rests down) and it's next to the door – so it's probably always down to avoid a trip hazard?. To engage or disengage the handbrake you pull it up, but then let it down, so it's hard to explain – you'll work it out in real life I'm sure.

- Then you get things like the instrument panels – nothing is exactly intuitive by its location – and then you notice the writing on the dials looks like it's from a cheap Chinese knock-off of Letraset, if you remember that excellent product from your school days. I forged many a dinner ticket at school for chums and I reckon did a better job than whoever made Aston dials a decade or so ago. I'm sure they're much better now but in the early models, in certain lights, the text literally looks like it's added as an afterthought as you can see in my photograph.

(Image courtesy Alamy)

So it's probably fair to say things weren't off to a flying start, then we had to sit for a while whilst the *gearbox and oil loosened-up a bit* (Ed – Technical term?). But then we started the test drive proper, once I'd plucked up enough courage to drive off the forecourt in **kangaroo** jumps of course as it's not as easy as you'd think.

I now knew why it takes a while for a car with a dry sump to get going!

Note to Editor

Dry Sump IS a technical term. The readers will get it even if you don't.

One thing I noticed within minutes was the attitude and approach of other road users and pedestrians: they seemed to be **reverential**. That's an odd word I know, especially for a car test drive, but immediately it was apparent people gave you courtesy, time and space on the road, apart from Audi drivers of course, but that's a given – and more about them in due course! And young lads on pavements, bicycles or in cars would go out of their way to **wave**, point or even give a **thumbs-up** sign as you roared past. Now that hadn't happened at all in the Maserati, which was odd – that car was just as lovely and almost as expensive.

However, all was not well. Remember the salesman who had lured me into this Aston as it was a manual transmission?

I just couldn't drive it – the clutch was so strong to push that after about ten minutes on the test drive, albeit on easy roads, I could feel my leg **muscles** starting to ache – this was certainly no Grand Tourer.

I sadly cut the test short and no matter how much I'd enjoyed the car, I felt it wasn't practical if I'd end up with leg strain on anything beyond a five-minute journey, so I put Aston also into the reject bin along with the Maserati.

So much for stupid goal boards!

And that was it for a while. I gave up on my dreams of getting a luxury car – I probably started thinking about the Espresso machine or buying a Kia Sorrento as the next target on my goal board!

Chapter 8

Down but not Out – I Haven't Given Up

However I simply couldn't forget those thumbs up and waves from passers by – the drive in the Aston Martin had left its marque (not that word again! Ed) so I started to scour the for sale adverts online looking a bit further afield further and researching more into Aston Martin as a brand.

I also decided to visit Aston Martin themselves at the site of the original **factory** in Newport Pagnell which is only about a 20-minute drive from home. I didn't get into the factory (as that's been moved to a green field site at Gaydon in Warwickshire and they're building a new mega factory in Wales right now) but on site they do restorations of James Bond classics, repairs, and of course sell new cars. If you've never been into an Aston Martin showroom I commend you to do so. Wall to wall marble, huge windows, spotless cars, you'll probably also get a free proper coffee as the staff are incredibly helpful and friendly. They are happy to chat, nothing is too much trouble and unlike a traditional car dealership they don't put you under any time pressure, even if it's clear you can't afford the car and are just window shopping. This was a world apart from the Maserati dealership in Nottingham who wouldn't even let me stand near their car. There they must have made a snap (incorrect) judgement that I couldn't afford the car and never would, whereas my experience of Aston is that they probably realise you might just be **motivated** enough to try if they help you a bit, so why not take time to encourage you?

Nice One Aston.

I was well and truly hooked, I had now narrowed down my choice of vehicle to an Aston V8 Vantage with **SportShift**, which is a sort of semi-automatic gearbox complete with flappy paddles on the steering wheel like an F1 car. I started tracking down a dealer for a test drive, this time, not a manual version. I wasn't hopeful that it would remedy my previous concerns about the car, but it was worth a go. I found a great car within a few weeks and a very willing dealer, Chiltern Aston, about an hour away down near Hemel Hempstead just outside London. So off I went, popping into a Jaguar dealership on the way (as the XK is a similar car with some common DNA to the Aston) for purposes of comparison, which seemed like a sensible idea and as I've said I wasn't letting go of my £40k+ lightly!

Again the Aston dealers were friendly and helpful, with no time pressure, and they let me have an hour's test drive, which again isn't that typical. These were an approved dealership but not actually owned by Aston Martin themselves, but it's the only marque of car they sell and work on.

Much to my surprise this time the car was an absolute delight, both visually, interior and out, it was also great to drive – it still took a few minutes for the engine and oil to warm up of course and all the aforementioned issues like upside down switches and Letraset were still present, but the pleasure of driving the car complete with its six speed auto change gearbox made up for all the issues.

NB. The newer cars have an even faster seven speed gearbox which apparently auto-changes more quickly. And in theory my car is even better to drive using only the manual flappy paddle shifts on the steering wheel, although I liked using the automatic function due to sheer laziness as an older driver.

Our test drive covered a mix of winding country roads, dual carriageways, and the famous or is it infamous, six-roundabouts-in-one-roundabout in Hemel itself, which I can confirm is a very scary prospect for your first time out in an Aston Martin. The noise from the engine was fantastic, the smell of the interior was absolutely lovely (if you like leather, and you know I do by now).

Editor's Note

Yes, we know you do!

So I was sold (or maybe a better phrase might be I'd been bitten and bought!) and I decided during the drive that I would try and negotiate a good deal, firstly with the dealership, and then with Mrs H (wife). It was made easier of course as I was a cash buyer and had no car to trade-in, so a deal could be done quickly. We commenced negotiations over another coffee back at the garage and agreed a price, from memory, about **5% below** the asking price, so not dissimilar to the kind of discount you might get when buying a house.

I subsequently discovered that with many garages selling luxury cars, due to the large costs of stock, they often don't acquire the cars and sell them on but take them on for a commission, so in effect it still belongs to the seller and the garage just take a modest fee for introducing you to each other. Once completed the sale paperwork does shift across to the garage itself as they will be the ones to honour whatever warranty is given. My car, being a bit newer, even came complete with a full **Aston-Martin warranty** for 12 months and a year's MOT when that became due so it truly was 99% like buying a new car, albeit about 70% cheaper.

Chapter 9

What Did I Get for My Money?

I have already waxed lyrically over the fact that the car looked **like new**, both inside and out, and mentioned that I believe it was a Press Car used originally by Aston when they launched the V8 Vantage. This meant it had an unusual colour scheme – paint that looked black (my preferred colour) from a distance but actually had a rather snazzy purple tinge on closer inspection and in certain lights. The leather interior was red of course, but had a hint of burgundy, and silver stitching, and this leather covers almost every surface (especially now I've added a bit more).

It was completed by a burgundy, thick velvet-pile carpet, a cream Alcantara headlining (which added to the *as new* smell), the aforementioned semi-automatic gearbox, electric mirrors, satellite navigation, heated seats, multi-change CD, auto-fold heated mirrors, tyre-monitoring, heated windscreen, cruise-control and that's about it. I tell a lie, it was also configured for an iPhone or iPad through a dangling wire in the glovebox, not the most glamorous way to add a feature but that's the quirkiness you grow to love in a car like this.

So it would be wrong to imply the car was stingy with extras but it didn't have as many features as my Alfa Romeo Brera (which cost about 25% of the Aston's price when new) and no doubt nowhere near as many as the beloved Nissan Maxima QX which costs about 30% of the new price. If I was looking for a car with memory seats, self-dipping lights, automatic tailgate, keyless entry, and more, then I needed to look elsewhere!

Actually whilst on this subject, to this day (six plus years into my Aston Martin ownership experience) I'm still not really sure if my car has fog lights! I can't find any button to press to make any special separate lights come on in fog, the manual is of course worse than useless as its written with so many options, and presumably countries, in mind, and I assume the headlights are in fact multi-purpose designed to work in all conditions? All I can say on that is it's a great shock when you get caught out in fog with no button to press and let's just say the lights aren't exactly *illuminating* under such conditions, but they are truly *brilliant* in normal weather.

Editor's Note

Before you ask, yes, we see what you did there.

As expected the seats are comfortable, the driving position is nice, and even though the picture below doesn't really convey the quality, you do have the pleasure of a clock that IMHO is so attractive it could be made into a wristwatch – and all that lovely leather.

Image courtesy Autocar

Chapter 10

Collection aka Planes Trains & Automobiles?

After a wait of a few weeks to give the garage time to complete a full service, MOT and free valet, and me time to arrange insurance it was time to collect the car, and I decided to make a big occasion out of it as this was a special day for me – achieving a goal, even if not the one I had originally set for myself. So I booked a day's holiday and made plans.

Editor's Note

Surely you don't need to book time off from your own business.

Author

You do if you live/work with organised females like I do.

Images courtesy Creative Commons

I opted for what I now call the **Planes, Trains & Automobiles Day** in homage to one of my favourite John Candy / John Hughes Movies. I didn't need to fly anywhere as the garage was only about 60 miles from home but I thought it would be a great contrast and hence a memorable experience to:

- Start the day on **foot** with a half mile walk to the bus stop (even though we have a nearer one)
- Then take the **bus** into Northampton, for around a thirty minute journey
- Then get the **train** from Northampton to Berkhamsted station about an hour away
- Then get picked up by the garage in a **chauffeur** driven Range Rover – it was actually the owner's car driven by one of his team who kindly ferried me the last ten miles or so through the Chiltern Hills.
- Then drive home in my **Aston Martin**, on cruise control and no speeding of course.

As you can probably imagine the journey home was a little tense, starting on small country roads, then round the notorious Hemel roundabout system and finally a motorway system chocker-block with every imaginable speed camera and temporary speed restriction, but it was worth it!

The plan took a day but was as expected, truly **memorable** and it made me appreciate the car even more by re-experiencing modes of transport I've had to use in the past, apart from a chauffeur of course.

Chapter 11

Tax & Insurance

I had of course done a few checks online before buying the car to get an idea regarding likely tax and insurance costs and it was a mix of good and not so good news, plus some big surprises.

Road tax is of course expensive as these cars are gas guzzlers, hence why mine is used mostly for short journeys (under 5 miles) and not anything over 10 miles, but I still get to use it most days. I suspect the overall environmental impact isn't as bad as people imagine as luxury cars tend not to get scrapped but live forever (Aston claim 90% of their cars ever made are still useable) so the environmental build-cost savings help subsidize the excessive impact of driving them, and surely manual workers are even more eco-friendly than robots? But irrespective of the truth, tax is currently around **£10 a week** and my thinking is if you can afford the car, you can afford the tax, and should pay it without grumbling.

Insurance isn't that easy to arrange as most normal insurers won't cover cars like this either individually or under a multicar policy, which surprised me, as plainly I can't drive two cars at once so I expected my Alfa insurer to gladly add this new car on. They wouldn't, at any price, and I think it's because of their limited knowledge about repairs rather than a cost thing.

The solution was simple, low cost and a great experience. I arranged my insurance through the Aston Martin Owners Club, which is certainly worth joining if only initially to get your name published in the Annual Year Book for posterity to show the grandchildren.

Membership costs about £30 a year for Aston owners although bizarrely is free for enthusiasts, maybe because they don't get in the aforementioned book! The events are worth a trip out too and they have regular, owners' meetings nationally, usually in a nice restaurant somewhere.

This cheap membership in turn enabled me to get a very good deal with specialist Aston-only insurance which was arranged via Lockton High-Net-Worth Insurance with the policy ultimately underwritten by Chubb, yes, that's Chubb of *locks-on-your-door* fame. And the premium, which is fully comprehensive, covers me for a value higher than the purchase cost, includes breakdown recovery and even things like driving on a track-day at Silverstone for less than **£2 a day**. That's double what my Alfa costs but a lot less than I was anticipating. The other pleasant surprise is you get to deal via real people with names, not anonymous call centres, there is minimal paperwork and not much small-print, and in short they treat you with respect akin to yesteryear which is a lovely surprise. The same applies to Claims, which I will cover if I remember to talk about the accident!

I've included below, courtesy of Parkers, an extract of some of these current costs for my Aston Vantage V8, although I'm not actually sure whether mine is the 4.3 or 4.7, I thought it was 4.5! It's interesting to see the lack of insurance cost which must allude to the fact that cover isn't available through *normal* channels.

Standard Trim					
Engine	Power (bhp)	0-60 mph (secs)	Fuel Economy (mpg)	Insurance Group	Road Tax (per annum)
+ 4.3 V8 Petrol	380 - 430	4.6 - 4.9	16 - 20	-	£305 - £535
+ 4.7 V8 Petrol	420	4.7 - 4.9	20 - 22	-	£535
+ 6.0 V12 Petrol	510	4.1	17	-	£535

Whilst on the subject of official data I can't help but comment on those fuel economy figures. From my experience my car averages around **14 miles** to the UK gallon, it can go as high as about 25 mpg on a long motorway run but drops to 5mpg if you accelerate hard, which most people will do from time to time, surely, or why buy the car?

Again my philosophy is if you can afford the car you can afford the fuel without griping and you can cut costs (and environmental impact) by doing less miles in the Aston.

Choosing an annual mileage of 3,000 instead of 5,000 also saved about 25% on my insurance costs.

Author's Note

I am concerned about the environment but not so concerned as to ban ownership or manufacture of luxury cars.

*In fact I've gone further and alleviated my concerns/guilty conscience by creating our own unique company scheme to **offset** all the carbon used by our marketing agency and its employees, including commuting and private mileage.*

So in theory at least my gas guzzling Aston Martin is in fact carbon neutral and maybe even greener than a new electric car.

Editor's Note

Sounds suitably quirky but cool, nice idea.

Chapter 12

Getting Home

I have already mentioned that my cars are kept in an alarmed garage. Parking the Aston Martin for the first time wasn't an experience for the faint hearted as this is a wide car and I have narrow garage gates, plus I'm not super-hot at gauging distances and widths. My solution was to buy LED lights from the local car accessory shop, I think they are meant for boy-racers to pimp their cars underneath, and for about £20 I was able to put LED strips on the up-and-over support frame (where it would catch the side of the car if I misjudged my entry) and power these from the 12-volt supply coming out of the garage's automatic door opener above. So now I can see in the mirrors a glow down the side of the car, helping me ensure I park it centrally. And touch wood, no bumps so far.

Good lighting is a must, and in my case it's also important to avoid the mess in my garage. It may be clean, dry and alarmed but tidy it isn't.

Editor's note

We know Mrs H (both of them) would agree on this point! And Mrs H (mum) adds, **He always was a messy little boy**.

Author's note

Thanks for the moral support everyone.

A few weeks back we had a gas board engineer in the house and he needed to borrow some tools to save time rather than revisit his depot, so my wife volunteered a trip with him to the work bench in the garage.

Aside from being surprised that the Aston, which was at home that day, was parked about two inches from my Mountain bike and squeezed in next to ladders and a pile of paint tins, he was shocked to discover a work bench one foot deep in discarded tools and the angle grinder that was fixed in situ pointing straight at the Aston's bonnet. Luckily my wife stood in the way to stop the stray sparks from hitting the car in case he was less than careful….

She must really love that car after all!

My point is this, it's a working garage and my working cars must fit in, but at least they are put away every night protected from the bad weather, if not from falling tools!

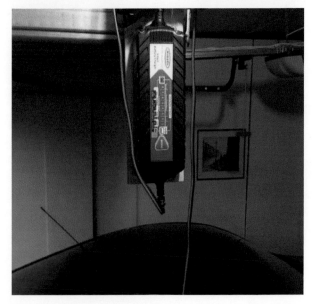

Given the problem these kinds of cars have re needing regular charging I had also taken the precaution of fitting a trickle charger suspended from the roof near the driver's door window, so it's nice and convenient to quickly put the battery on charge.

Author's note

Before the Editor comments, yes, I have pictures in that untidy garage!

Editor's note

I see you removed the beach babes photo before the photoshoot?

Chapter 13

Surprised Reactions – People you Know & Car Brands

Ok, so you've bought an Aston Martin and safely got it home, now is the time you'd expect to be able to look forward to the reactions of your friends and family, people who've seen you struggle through life to make ends meet and then go a step further to achieve one of your goals.

Right?

No, Wrong.

If my experience is anything to go by, one of the most interesting things about buying a luxury car like an Aston Martin is that you can't predict how people will **react**, and it may surprise you a lot when so-called friends who you expected might be most positive, (perhaps at point B in the chart below) turned out to be almost rude and behave as if the car was invisible, in one famous case even claiming *never to have heard of Aston Martin* even though they were a big James Bond/007 fan!

At the other end of the spectrum there were of course many friends who were pleased and some so much so that they even wanted to go for an immediate spin around the block. Mrs H (my mum this time) was one of these, even though she's well past retirement age but I obviously can't say by how much!

Neighbours, whom you might reasonably expect to have been a little bit negative due to being competitive (assuming keeping up with the Joneses and all that is a real thing) were uniformly pleased and positive. Work

colleagues (who could have been a bit miffed at seeing such an obviously visible sign that you were doing OK) were also extremely supportive rather than a reaction somewhere like the following (A in the diagram below) which was expected. I had asked staff to guess about the marque once they'd realised why I'd booked my day's holiday for a *Planes, Trains, Automobiles* day and of all the brands they thought I might be buying, Aston wasn't even on the list as these cars are deemed out of everyday reach I think. I can remember the surprised faces to this day when I turned up with the car in real life. They were plainly shocked – again I think this is because of the brand's perceived costs being higher than actual costs.

Finally I should mention **clients**. I had previously thought that if you provide any service to people who may visit your premises then it's surely best to leave an Aston Martin or any luxury car at home so as not to create any suspicion, however unwarranted, that you might **overcharge**?

Editor's Note

Presumably a reverse theory of it being a good idea only ever hiring a plumber or decorator in a rundown van as they offer cheap prices (but may in fact be running a Ferrari at home!)?

This hasn't been born out of experience and overall clients have been neither positive nor negative so I can't decide if knowledge of ownership has impacted the business or not.

I suspect not. In most cases I leave it at home anyway on days when we might get a visit, just to be safe and avoid the risk of upsetting any apple carts.

The chart below maps out how I have noticed most people's reactions over a six year period, influenced of course by the extent or otherwise to which I consider them a car nut or not being in the slight bit interested in cars – my theory being if they like any cars, they should be more likely to show an interest?

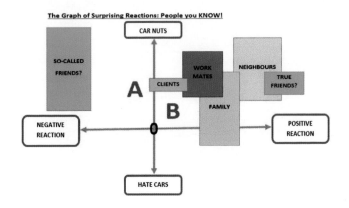

The Graph of Surprising Reactions: People you KNOW!

The reactions of other road users are also worthy of comment and probably even worthy of a psychological study by high paid academics on the tax payers' payroll.

I was so surprised by this aspect of ownership in the first few weeks that I started carrying around a **Dictaphone** to note down experiences, and this formed the start of this book – you may be suitably surprised yourself.

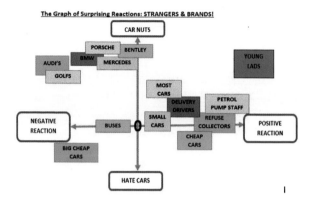

The Graph of Surprising Reactions: STRANGERS & BRANDS!

First off I must comment on the **Positive Reactions** of the lovely people who staff our **refuse lorries** – I have now bumped (**Editor's note** – hopefully not literally!) into them several times when filling up the car at various petrol stations around the county and in about 80% of cases they can be relied upon to **go out of their** way to talk about the Aston and say something positive to me. They like to chat about fuel consumption, what it's like to drive, and so on. I have no idea whether they are paid more than we might think and are all secretly saving up to buy an Aston but from the way they react there is certainly no hint of jealousy or anything of that ilk.

If only I could say the same for drivers of some of the up-market-brand cars, but more about them in a moment!

Staff at the aforementioned **garages/petrol stations** also probably comment in about 50% of cases, usually saying Astons are their favourite cars. So it's a good conversation starter but they only tend to say anything when the garage is otherwise empty!

Young lads giving a smile and a thumbs up we have already encountered during the test drive stage and this persists through my 6 years of ownership with something like this happening at least once a **week** – although my wife claims never to have noticed when she is in the car, so maybe it's all actually a figment of my imagination? Without wishing to be sexist I can't recall any young girls even noticing at all, never mind a wave or thumbs up, but maybe that's a stereotype that will be fixed with future generations now that boys will probably soon only be allowed to wear dresses for school and girls can only become firemen, sorry, fire-persons, in an increasingly PC world?

The **smaller** and less impressive an approaching car is the more likely the other drivers appear to be extra courteous, even pleased to see an Aston-Martin on the road alongside them and, if it's possible to judge, respectful of your ownership, and I measure this via the extent to which they will smile or wave, let you have right of way, irrespective of whether it is your right of way, that kind of thing. This also applies to most **delivery drivers** in white-vans, but presumably is easier to explain – they want to avoid the hassle of an expensive bump and explaining it to the boss so they sit and wait rather than the more usual pushing through that gap!

Negative and even aggressive reactions, such as *noticeably* pushing in when in a queue of traffic or rushing through a gap even when they clearly **don't** have right of way seems to be sadly a typical reaction of a large proportion (as much as 30%) of drivers of more luxurious vehicles, headed up by a minority of what I term **Audi Asses** and boy-racers in VW **Golfs.** So whilst Audi drivers are by far the worst offenders in this regard (are they rude to everyone?) it was a noticeable reaction amongst the drivers of what, on reflection, were predominantly luxury German cars such as BMW, Mercedes and Porsche who rarely give any courtesy on the road. It led me to conclude that in an Aston Martin you begin to feel like a lone Tommy in your trusty Spitfire against the might of the approaching Blitzkrieg!

Editor's Note

Tommies relate to the 1st World War and Blitzkrieg the 2nd, plus we doubt if BMW. Porsche, or Mercedes, whatever the model, come complete with air back-up!

Bus drivers are of course generally pretty difficult with everyone and the drivers of **large cheap cars**, like the **Chrysler 300C**/Bentley copy can also be generally relied upon to employ bully boy tactics – whereas real Bentley owners and even the odd Range Rover driver are normally pretty accommodating. After long consideration I think I've decided it's all equivalent to playing Top Trumps – people who have got themselves a nice car and are visibly doing well in life, at the top of the greasy pole you might say, don't like to be reminded they could have tried harder!

The reaction of these other road users, particularly the aggressive ones, is, I think, one of the very **best things** about owning one of these lovely cars. If it helps put a few people back in their box: how can that be such a bad thing, whatever the fuel economy? Obviously I also need to apologise in advance to anyone who knows me who has one of the aforementioned brands – my comments aren't levelled at them I'm sure, unless they know differently how they react!

Chapter 14

Special Days – Everyday, Weddings, Accidents, The Tunnel & Winding Roads

In addition to all of these interesting reactions from other people, we have had many lovely days out in the Aston and several memorable ones, as these examples might show.

Everyday use puts a smile on my face but my wife hates it (she doesn't drive) as she doesn't like fast acceleration. It's certainly a good end to a bad day when you use an Aston for your commute home and sometimes it's hard to stop yourself taking a journey that is just a little bit further than necessary.

Editor's Note

As a meanie I'm sure you manage to fight this urge most days!

We went to a couple of **Owners' Club** events at stately homes. Obviously, it's a super experience being ushered in via a dedicated *Aston Only* entrance and parking your car amongst rows of similar cars, most of course costing many times more. To be honest the owners' meetings are a bit too geeky for me, as I don't polish every nut and bolt on the car every day, but plenty of people enjoy that sort of thing. We went expecting to find loads of fun stalls selling accessories, jackets and more besides, just like we'd experienced 30 years earlier at a Mini extravaganza, so we were shocked at the lack of commercialism surrounding one of the world's best known and most treasured brands.

If I had time now would be a good place to mention that I also like watches, owning about a dozen, and I fancied getting an Aston branded one, similar to my Alfa Romeo chronograph. Does such a thig exist? Well if it does I've never found it although many watch brands associate themselves with Aston and advertise in the official Aston magazine, but none (until recently with the DBS) put the logo or any relevant branding on their watch faces. I would tell you I even got as far as contacting Aston and volunteering to oversee setting up such a product, but not surprisingly they didn't bother replying. Ditto with pens, but I did manage to find a half decent one either from the Aston official magazine or the owners' club. To be honest it's at best OK but probably not the quality you would expect from such a great brand. Anyway, we haven't got time for that diversion.

The **Wedding**. The daughter of long-standing family friends was getting married from home and it turned out her fiancé was a real James Bond 007 nut, so it was always his dream to get married in an 007 type car. Now whilst my particular V8 isn't exactly the same as say a Db9 or a Vanquish used in recent films, it has the same design DNA and was considered appropriate so I got the pleasant request for a favour to be chauffeur for the day ferrying the groom back and forth between home, church and reception. Here's Martin, the groom, looking the part whilst having a minute's rest from photographers and fighting terrorists at an icy lair somewhere.

Editor's Note

Surely with that registration this belongs to someone like Simon Cowell?

Author's Note

Watch it! I'll talk about that in a minute!

The **Accident** has been mentioned several times already and it was certainly memorable, for mostly the wrong reasons. I'd decided to take Mrs H (the wife) for a leisurely Sunday drive to a local garden centre about ten miles away. After a nice coffee we meandered back to the car and carried on chatting. The car park was nearly empty as the garden centre had closed so we reversed out slowly, too slowly as it happened. Rear visibility isn't a strong point on most of the modern Astons and mine is no exception, so I didn't see a new Audi A8 fast approaching us (as you can see almost nothing through the rear windows) and when I'd checked the mirrors, perhaps a minute earlier, nobody was coming. I missed him and he missed seeing my reversing lights, so ploughed into us at about 30mph. The bang was horrendous but luckily nobody was injured. The front of the Audi collapsed and all air bags went off. On the Aston the bumper was cracked and the boot popped up about a centimetre, but otherwise everything seemed OK. The other driver was friendly. I think he thought it was his fault, as he didn't slow down at a stop sign 100 yards previous. This is when the memorable bit started.

I went to contact my insurers the next day only to discover my MOT had just expired a few days earlier. I **had** got a date booked in with the garage but I had incorrectly assumed it was legal to drive in the interim and that a car without a valid MOT is still insured, I now gather that may **not** be the case in the UK, and I was in fact uninsured as the car wasn't deemed legal to drive. This is before the accident. It was certainly less fit afterwards!

Anyway, I expected a real bun fight with the insurers, but they were absolutely chilled, took everything in their stride, got the car fixed and paid for both vehicles (it was deemed my fault as I was the one reversing, even though we had strong video evidence to show the other party was more careless and speeding) with no fuss and no palaver of any kind.

The insurers were fantastic.

More about the accident.

On closer investigation of the car immediately after the accident I discovered some more damage in the boot, the carpet had been pushed up and underneath an aluminium honeycomb panel had buckled – it was like a cardboard box to look at but fabricated out of aluminium. For a brief moment I even considered knocking it back down with a builder's brick hammer to see if it would make the boot go back to its old level and shut properly! I decided not to and the following day hot-tailed it to a local repair garage that did good jobs touching up the Alfa from time to time, and I knew they worked on Land Rovers and Range Rovers, which also sometimes had strange manufacturing methods using aluminium, composite materials and even glue in place of welding. A repair that might have cost say £500 on a *normal* car was going to cost me £3,000 if it was a private job. I thought *ouch* but if I was indeed uninsured, that could of course have ended up a whole lot worse.

I then decided to take a trip down to the Aston dealers where I'd first bought the car from so I could get a real price from an authorised garage, I was expecting £5,000, but instead what they said shocked me. They advised they **couldn't repair it** at all as it was a category A accident – obviously worrying as in general use a category A car is so badly damaged it has to be taken off the road and crushed, never to return! Luckily for me I learnt that this was some kind of strange internal Aston Martin coding system and it was actually a category D accident which can be repaired, but my usual specialist Aston garage weren't specialist enough or authorised by Aston to repair it. So they said they'd get an approved repairer to contact me.

Imagine my surprise a day or so later to get a call out of the blue which literally went something like this: "Hello mate, I hear you've got a problem with an Aston?"

It had all the makings of Arthur Daly Under-The-Arches Motors or a PPI scam telephone call so I was immediately on my guard and said: "Are you sure you are qualified to mend this kind of accident?

The response was even more shocking – the caller replied: "We should be, we built it in the first place!"

My caller was from the Aston Martin factory and they were calling on behalf of Aston Martin Works, the factory's own garage and restoration arm. They came out to check the car, provided a price estimate of £12,000, which was a shock versus other repairers, and this was after leaving out certain options – for example, I opted to blend in the repainting rather than respray most of the body.

Given the extent of the damage which was confined to the bumper, I trusted they could match that without even spraying any of the car itself. This proved to be correct and saved a few £thousand otherwise the bill would have been nearer £20k.

The next task was explain all this to the insurer – they were happy for me to **choose any option**, that is find a cheaper authorised repairer that wasn't the factory, or go back to the factory even if it was more than double the cost. Needless to say I picked the latter as it would make the car more saleable later knowing the factory that built it had brought it back to life and I'd end up with Aston Works Registration plates on the car to replace the originals.

The repairs took about a month, I assume as they are snowed under with work on proper restoration jobs not minor shunts, and upon completion it would be fair to say they'd done an OK job but not a great job. I had agreed as part of the work they would also quickly respray a couple of scratches near the rear lights and the door sill plates, I call them kick plates, as these regularly get damaged by careless passengers.

The Works conveniently forgot this extra work, ironic given their name, plus somehow made the **petrol cap release mechanism** stick – I suspect it's actually a bit of a design flaw on the Vantage but mine was fine until the Works somehow worked their magic on my car, or it could be coincidence.

I have since devised a widget that fixes it – punch a hole in an old credit card, attach it to a zip tie plus add a bit of blue-tack on the end for exuberance. The card will help the flap open if it is loosely slipped in the seam/gap; the tie and blue tack stop it falling to the ground.

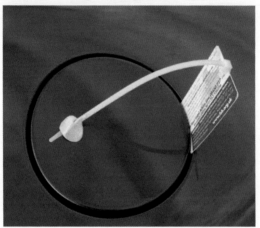

Patent Pending?

On the plus side the car was back on the road almost as good as new, plus I now had the aforementioned Aston Works branded number plates which as any 007 fan will agree are almost as sought after as Department Q.

The Tunnel – If like me you are a fan of Top Gear and similar motoring shows you'll have seen the clips whereby

Jeremy Clarkson or some other lucky devil gets to drive a performance car through a long road tunnel or under the Kremlin or other huge building with a big basement – and all in search of that illusive *special tunnel noise*.

I think I'd like to trademark that as a search term!

Well it just so happens that 40 miles from home in Leicester, where I grew up and attended University (or Polytechnic as it was in those days), there is a short but unusual curved underpass. So one day when we were visiting Mrs H (the mum) I decided to take Mrs H (the wife) on an unexpected 5 mile detour to said tunnel. I was suitably excited beforehand, obviously Mrs H thought I'd just gone mad as I probably hadn't revealed the intended destination and was just embarking on a mystery tour when we had places to be.

She soon changed her mind though. The first time through the tunnel, which I think was the slightly longer route, we dropped the windows, roared through (within the speed limit of course) and really the effect was nothing special. Mrs H wanted the windows back up so as to avoid messing with her hair but I persuaded her to let me try the return trip back down the other side, the slightly shorter route through the underpass. This time the sound track was absolutely **awesome** and I had redeemed myself, well a bit, but you'll probably never get her to admit it!

The **Winding Road** – We could of course go on a road trip to the Stelvio Pass (now immortalised as the name of the latest Alfa Romeo) to enjoy a great winding road but being a meanie, I tend to look a little nearer to home for a lovely Sunday drive and luckily one such route lies between our home and my mum's, so that's between Northampton and Leicester. It's actually the B6047, a country road from just north of Market Harborough (behind the McDonalds), so you can grab a coffee before setting off towards Billesdon, where it joins the A47.

This is a popular route with motorbikes too and hence as you'd expect it's not the safest road in the county but it is one of the best to drive in any vehicle that enjoys corners and being glued to the road, so great in an Aston or an Alfa and a lot cheaper to get to than the Italian Alps!

I don't actually drive the Aston as hard on these kinds of roads as I might the front wheel drive Alfa as to be absolutely honest I've never dared test it to the limits to learn how far you can push the traction and everything else before it allegedly corrects itself. Better to be safe than sorry.

Too Posh to Push (or drive)

I remember vividly the first day I tried to use my Aston in really inclement weather during my first few months of ownership – I'd bought it in the winter. I don't mean to suggest we'd had blizzards and metre high snow drifts but overnight around 1cm of snow had fallen. I confidently went to reverse the car out of the garage and literally the second the wheel hit the snow, the car refused to come out any further into the cold. I assume this was caused by the traction control, and if I'd accelerated a bit harder it might have overcome the problem – I chose not to push it, and went to work in the Alfa!

Chapter 15

Not So Special Days – Wheels, Sandpaper, Noises, Magnets, Dashboards & Batteries

I have already alluded to some of the not so special days above, but here are some specifics that spring to mind.

Damaged wheels – my car had pristine alloys upon delivery to me so imagine the horror when *doing-the-right-thing* visiting a poorly friend only to have squeezed through a narrow gap in a village street, I curbed the passenger wheel! I did take the car to a professional garage to get the wheel repaired but after 12 months the paint was lifting so I ended up inventing my own weird technique for wheel repairs!

It goes like this, firstly I wash the tyre then paint it with black tyre paint. Then I use newspaper to stuff the wheel cavity (covering the brake callipers) and cover the surrounding body panels, and use masking tape on the wheel logo and tyre valves. I sand the damage, fill any scratches and dents with epoxy filler, sand again, and then respray the wheel with primer and then alloy coloured paint. Inevitably some overspray will go onto the tyre and I cover this at the end with a final coat of black wheel paint, so I'm covering silver with black, not trying to clean off the silver or mask it so perfectly that there is no overspray. I've discovered this process delivers a more robust finish than the professional repair, is quicker and easier than trying to mask around the tyre (as not much sticks to rubber and grease) and the overspray will eventually degrade or drop off provided you remember the first all-important coat of tyre black or you'll ruin expensive tyres that only cost about £350 each!

The Sandpaper Monster - I have already owned up to squeezing my Aston into a working garage complete with paint tins and ladders. What I didn't have time to mention was that I also leave it in situ when embarking on DIY jobs at home!

Editor's note

Mrs H (the wife) says increasingly rare DIY jobs

I often attempt to squeeze by the car to reach drills and other tools. On this famous occasion I was doing a decorating task and squeezed by the car forgetting I had got sheets of sandpaper sticking out of my back pocket. To my absolute horror this grazed the bodywork near the rear light and as you'd expect it wasn't a fine grade of wet-and-dry paper but new sheets of the coarsest stubbiest paper you could find. So a few deep scratches were added to the car. I then hurried off to get some T-Cut and other wonder polishes from the other side of the garage, which necessitated squeezing down the other side of the car. And yes, you've guessed it, I scratched that side too, in exactly the same spot in exactly the same way. So I had scratches in the mirror image of the first!

Luckily I had some spare purple/blue/black paint in the garage (which I ended up using to respray the sill plates myself) so a light dusting of that combined with some careful polishing has made the slight damage almost completely invisible unless of course you know it's there. So the car's a bit more lived in now but almost back to normal, despite Aston Works forgetting to fix it.

The Funny Noise – this event really sticks in my memory as with hindsight it's so funny. I was happily driving along a country lane on a summer's day when I dropped the window to enjoy the engine roar. A few minutes later I hear a high pitched warning squeal coming from somewhere. I pull in to a layby, the noise still continues, I switch the engine off, the noise continues, so I'm a bit puzzled. I look in the manual but again it doesn't give away any clues, so I continue on my way as the car is otherwise driving and handling perfectly. I get to work, park up, switch off the car and go into the office, confident the alert will have stopped when it's time to go home seven or so hours later. When it's time to go, I get in the car, the noise is still happening, a bit quieter perhaps but there is no mistaking an alarm. It's just before closing time so I try contacting the local Aston dealer for advice, No, it's not a fault they've ever encountered before. So before going home and trying to see the impact of disconnecting the battery (made no difference to the noise!), I decide to record the alarm sound on my phone and email it overnight to my normal dealership in Hemel and the customer service helpline at Aston Martin themselves.

Not surprisingly Aston Martin weren't overly helpful – it's fair to say they are at their best when you are parting with a fortune, and they really are fantastically helpful then – but the dealership came back the next day and said they'd played the sound to the main mechanic, and he too couldn't identify the fault and had never heard that alarm before. So I agreed to take the car over to them. I was just preparing for my 60 mile journey when I noticed a small red warning light glowing down near the driver's door, but it wasn't from the car itself, but from my old **Dictaphone** which I had stored in the door – coincidentally it was there to record thoughts as they happened for this book!

I picked up the handset and realised not only was it glowing red but it was emitting a noise eerily similar to the warning noise coming from the Aston. It was of course the very same noise as it was coming from the Dictaphone, NOT the car. I must have knocked the recorder on when closing the door or messing with the windows a couple of days before and the noise and warning light were intended to warn me that the recorder had reached the end of the tape and it needed turning over.

I never did own up to the garage, it would be too embarrassing!

When is a magnet not a magnet? Some years previously I had noticed that luxury cars, despite having ample budget to afford it, are usually supplied without any kind of ding protection, and yet the very cheapest cars always come complete with this protection included. It's most odd and probably all down to aesthetics.

So I thought *why not invent a removable ding strip* that the owners of luxury cars can deploy in car-parks, stations and elsewhere. I came up with a couple of patentable ideas, sourced a manufacturer and made my prototype, which was magnetic. I tested it on my Alfa Romeo and was pleased to see it even stayed in place at 70mph, so would be safe even if you forgot to remove it. Imagine then my huge disappointment when I finally achieve my goal of acquiring an Aston Martin only to try and fit the device to the door and learn it won't stick – as the door isn't made from metal! I'm not sure what it's made from but I do know magnets don't like it! It was back to the drawing board – but at least another patentable idea resulted and this is in progress.

Dashboard Warnings – I've noticed that after a period of hard driving it's not uncommon to get a warning light come on. This will be usually for something you can't diagnose in the unhelpful and confusing manual, and of course Aston Customer Service aren't that disposed to help either as they want to drive you, not literally, to the main Dealers. I decided it wasn't fair to keep troubling my local dealers by phone so instead invested £20 in **a OBD11** Fault code reader which tells you what's wrong and often lets you reset the code with ease. By using this in combination with Google and helpful Aston Forums, it's possible to reduce your stress and reset codes that *appear when the car is run too hard or not hard enough*. Obviously for anything major it's still important to consider going to the garage but this simple device has taken a lot of stress out of ownership and teaches you that unlike a mass-produced car, where every light probably does mean a major fault, with a hand built car they are prone to daily hiccups and its vital not to stress over everything as a fault one day will often fix itself the next.

And a tool like this lets you reset the codes so otherwise you'd forever be in the dealership running up small and not so small bills for unnecessary work.

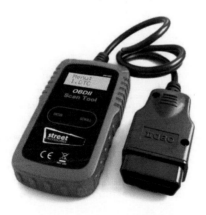

Image courtesy Euro Car Parts

The **Battery** – I'm not sure if it's a common occurrence with all large engine luxury cars, I assume so as they often seem to come equipped with specialist trickle battery chargers, but they do seem to discharge quickly if left unused and even after a few days a loss of power is noticeable. In the case of my car, as I use it for short journeys only, I've noticed that every time I start it, it seems to lose around 0.5 volts from the battery. Electricians will tell you this is impossible of course, but I think the car generally runs at about 14.5 volts and won't start once it's below 11 volts as it's such a huge heavy engine to turn over cold. So that's just a week's worth of starts and in cold weather it won't charge up enough to make up for this shortfall as you are also using heaters, window demisters and other electrical drains on the battery.

When it has **insufficient** charge the cars electronic systems make one hell of an unusual racket with all manner of alarms going off and to say it puts you off your dinner, lunch and breakfast is no exaggeration – it sounds like a very expensive fault and is one of the most distressing noises I've ever heard in my life, even worse than a baby crying!

In practice, the car may need nothing more than a slow charge overnight. I have resolved this problem in three ways, firstly fitting a **new battery** of the highest power output recommended, secondly, I have left wires in place permanently so I now have a charging socket easily located behind the driver's seat and can put the car on charge in about 60 seconds versus the usual hassle of lifting the flap behind the seats and locating the battery. And I have then wired up my own version of a voltmeter which cost about £5 for parts (a switch and display) and I have then covered this in matching leather and placed it in the driver's footwell. So I can simply switch this on when I think the battery may be getting a little tired. If its anywhere near 11volts when the engine is off, I know it needs charging soon.

Yes, that's matching leather!

PS. I'm convinced the car is actually built around the battery as it's nigh on impossible to get it out of the car – a piece of aluminium trim (on an Aston even hidden trim is lovingly crafted out of aeroplane grade materials) has to slide to one side but won't quite go far enough. From memory I had to force it and then cut 1cm off to make it easier to refit and remove in future.

Chapter 16

Living with an Aston Martin

As an outsider looking in it's so easy to assume that living with an Aston Martin as your day car is a ludicrous proposition and hugely expensive. Whilst it's true in part, in general this hasn't been borne out by my own real life experiences as follows:

- **Insurance** – as already mentioned this is barely any different to a decent specification *normal* car.
- **Servicing** – it's a little more expensive if you go to Aston Martin dealerships but if you go to the approved specialist dealers around the country it's surprisingly affordable to get a service – costs are typically in in the £600-£800 range….so probably only 40% premium to most cars.
- **Tyres** – these are expensive so need to be looked after. They are such huge tyres, and you are supposed to fit one brand which I think is Bridgestone at around £350 a tyre, but much to the consternation of Aston Martin I fit the same specification / speed rating on Continentals or Pirelli and get the cost down to a much more manageable £250 each, but still 60% or so more than most cars.
- **Warranties** – these can be obtained for around £100 a month. I had one initially but opted instead to forget this and just put the money saved towards

future repairs. In six years, nothing major has been necessary so I've saved this money.

- **Repairs** – things like brakes (see below) can be repaired pretty reasonably for a few £hundred, items like a clutch are expensive at around £2000. However I learnt a good trick here – if you switch the car on and off about twenty times (not a full start or you won't have any battery left!) then it recalibrates many of the systems, and this seems to happen with the clutch too. I had originally thought I needed a new one in the first six months of ownership and six years on, it's still going strong so cost = £nil.
- **Parking** – with such a wide car this becomes a bit more tricky, either because you might struggle (like me) to keep the car within the irritatingly narrow concrete kerbs that so easily damage wheels, or you won't find a space wide enough or next to a well-cared for car that doesn't look likely to ding your bodywork. Cost nil but the hassle factor might irate a passenger if you make them walk further and park 100 yards further away, as I do.
- **Consumables** – that's things like oil. These are no more expensive than any high performance car per litre, but with such a big engine the amounts consumed are large so you may end up doubling the typical cost so that's around £120 extra on every service.
- **Brake Pads** – this may be a function of my driving style or the fact that in an Aston some of the aforementioned aggressive drivers we've talked about seem to delight in forcing you to brake more often than a normal car, but it seems true to say the

Aston is heavy on its brakes, for example versus my Alfa which covers more miles, so expect to allow an extra £5-10 per week, depending on mileage, for this kind of consumable every service too.

- **Breakdown Cover** – this is less expensive as its bundled in for free with the Insurance.

Aside from costs there are of course other things that only come to life when you actually own anything and live with it day to day. An Aston Martin is no exception:

- **Build Quality** – you will be able to see little blemishes that aren't apparent in say a mass-produced vehicle built mostly by robots. Depending on your perspective they will be either endearing (serving as a reminder of old fashioned craftsmanship) or be alarming given the cost. So for example, whilst the interior is stunning in every way, you can't help but feel under all the leather the dashboard is fashioned out of plywood and timber. The car body panels won't fit the same everywhere, so as an example a gap between panels or the bonnet and boot may be 2mm greater on one-side of the car than the other. To me these quirks add character – I remember a Ferrari dealer telling me years ago that they need to respray parts of nearly every new car they receive from the factory!
- **Touching Up** – one way you can help maintain the car's quality is always be ready to touch up any minor blemishes – a downside is that even armed with the colour codes, you won't find these paints available at your usual Halfords or car accessory

shop, and the same applies to most of the fluids, windscreen wiper blades and such like. (Although you can sometimes get away with trial and error and Land Rover or Volvo parts). I solved the paint problem by alerting the dealer to a small problem early on and they kindly posted me a small jar of paint. It is normally possible to get an acceptable colour match on leather paints online, presumably these are a slightly less precise match than body panels, so for around £20 you can easily equip yourself to care for the interior.

- **Forget DIY Servicing** – so much of the mechanics of the car, including the engine, is hidden away that it's almost impossible to find anything on the car that is in an accessible place to check or work on yourself. So the key for me is find a good garage who can look after it regularly, on time, at an acceptable price without adding on unnecessary extras. And don't visit them unless you really need too!

- **Sprucing Up** – one thing it is good to consider doing yourself of course, aside from the usual oil and tyre pressure checking, are little tasks to tidy up the car, so that could be the wheels, respraying the metal wiper arms (as these seem to deteriorate quicker than the car bodywork in general) and on my own Vantage, for some reason, the small metal strips separating what I think are called the quarter-lights on the doors, had also tarnished so benefited from an easy to apply coat of matt black.

- **The Driving Experience** – driving an Aston really does make you feel special and it's impossible not to feel as if you have achieved something in life, even if that's a bit crass. However, from an actual driving perspective you will also discover the cars are noisy, unforgiving on bumpy roads, so scary on bends that only the brave will test whether they really are as forgiving as they say, rear visibility is poor, and I'd say they're not so great on long journeys (ignoring the fuel economy) on anything bar perfect roads like motorways. On the plus side they have great brakes, really bright lights and the soundtrack from the hi-fi or from the engine really is something to behold. And of course acceleration is almost as extreme as you can imagine – I describe it as being on a par with a motorcycle or riding a big dipper ride at an amusement park – but you also get creature comforts and the smell of leather in that stunning interior!

- **Mind your head –** it takes a particular talent to duck and swivel in just the right manner to get in and out of an Aston without you or your passenger banging their head, so take it slow the first few times and remember a**e first. Perhaps it's a good idea to put your hand above prospective passengers' heads as you kindly hold the door open for them!
- **The Boot –** or lack of. Aston have, I think, made a virtue out of the fact that you can fit a set of golf clubs in the boot of a Vantage. It's probably true (I've only tried a half set) but you won't get much else in if you're thinking of combining golf and a little road trip to a nice hotel. Likewise family food shopping will be a squeeze and of course there is little spare space behind the front seats. Other points of note regarding the Aston boot are:

- It's heavy – and that's despite being made no doubt out of aluminium or some kind of advanced composite. So make sure the gas struts that support it are working.

- The emergency release toggle in the boot itself is easily broken.

- Many Vantages have a leaky boot – often due to blocked drain holes – mine never has, but it's an obvious design quirk that when lifting the boot after rain, whatever water is on the lid and window will end up depositing itself on you and your luggage.

- **The Magazines** – if you are lucky, Aston Martin will add you onto the mailing list of their AM Owners magazine for free. It's a very stylish affair full of aspirational articles suitable for billionaires and an associated array of advertising for products no sane mortal can or would afford. Much more down to earth is the over-the-counter magazine *Vantage* published by Dennis Publishing, available to everyone by subscription or individually for around £3 and it's a good magazine to give you a feel for the cars, used prices, spares and garages and a whole lot more besides. It also includes aspirational advertising but is a bit more achievable on the goal board. And finally the Owners' Club, who are a nice friendly bunch, albeit IMHO a bit car obsessed but then I guess that's the point of an Owners Club, who publish the AM Quarterly magazine which is more **Event, Road-Trip** and **Restoration** focused. I enjoyed all the magazines for different reasons but one thing they have in common is they remind you it's an absolute privilege to feel you belong to a small and exclusive club – in the UK only around 0.03% of car drivers have an Aston Martin and this drops to just 1 in 20,000 people globally, which is circa **0.002%.** You don't get much more exclusive than that. NB. I assume I received the Aston Martin AM magazine as I had previously used the Works for my repairs rather than based on any wealth or fame criteria!

AM
THE ASTON MARTIN MAGAZINE

Zest of a
wave
THE ARCTIC SURFERS IN SEARCH
OF THE ULTIMATE THRILL

Images courtesy Aston Martin, My Subs and the Owners Club.

Editor's Note

Apparently only around 65,000 Aston Martins have been built, most of which are still road-worthy!

Author's note

You are a very knowledgeable man on pretty much everything!

- **Mind Your Age** – as even a pre-loved Aston can look like new, especially as they make so few changes to the range (and only enthusiasts will be so familiar with the brand as to know exactly what you are driving) it's tempting to be able to mind your age and fool the world with a personalised number plate. As you would expect, especially due to the 007 connection, almost every decent number has gone or will cost you more than the car itself, maybe even more than a new Aston. Hence why people think my car is owned by a Simon!

Author's note

Before the Editor comments rudely I will let you in on a secret. My plan was to try and find a Country Code sticker for the A (so probably Australia or Antarctica) and then space out my plate S7 ONM, with the 7 straightened, so on a personalised plate (sorry, show plate) it would look something like below. Needless to say, it's not perfect, but hopefully you get the idea and it only cost about £400!

Editor's Note

*What can I say other than **Austria** and they saw you coming!*

Chapter 17

Actual Running Costs

Whilst I'm not so sad as to write down every single bill and petrol receipt I do keep a pretty good handle on most costs, so for example, I can recall that when I fully calculated the costs of owning a previous car of mine, a new Vauxhall Cavalier, almost **30 years ago,** it was over £200 a month or **£2,500** a year, then. So with this as a benchmark and using approximate figures for fuel economy, fuel cost per litre and past road tax rates, it's interesting to see what good value the Alfa Brera represents at around £350 a month, all in, today. Allowing for inflation this should have increased to £660 a month.

		Aston Martin V8 Vantage		Alfa Romeo Brera 2.4 Diesel
First Acquired		12-Jan-12		01-Nov-10
Mileage Covered		**18,305**		**55,455**
Depreciation	£	11,500	£	12,700
Petrol/Diesel (Estimate)	£	7,017	£	9,663
Service/MOT/Repairs	£	6,205	£	3,465
Insurance / Breakdown Cover	£	3,498	£	2,765
Road Tax (Estimate)	£	2,106	£	1,540
Tyres	£	965	£	1,400
Insurance Excess re Claim	£	250	£	-
Cost Per Annum	**£**	**5,069**	**£**	**4,250**
Cost Per Mile	**£**	**1.72**	**£**	**0.57**
Monthly Cost	£	422	£	354 £ 777

NB. Figures from the AA suggest per mile costs of **£2.12** & **£0.54** for cars of this value / type.

What I find particularly interesting is that whilst the Aston Martin costs per mile are significantly higher due primarily to fuel economy and service/garage/brake costs, this is **offset** to a degree by a lower depreciation ratio as this is no higher than a *normal* car like the Brera.

Editor's note

Firstly we wouldn't consider a Brera a normal everyday car, secondly, surely Alfas are known for their sky high depreciation, So that's the worst car to compare to?

Author's note

That sounds like Mrs H (wife) saying our practical car isn't practical even if It has 4 seats and a hatchback! Re depreciation, whilst it's true Alfas do tend to devalue a little quicker than most cars, over a 7 year ownership period on a now 10 year old car, the actual difference is minimal vs the average, as over 10 years the value in most cars will have eroded away. As you can see, despite the much higher car value, the depreciation (as a %) is a lot lower on the Aston Martin and almost the same in absolute £ terms. Luxury and classic cars do maintain value better and may even go up in value in later years.

It should be noted that whilst my Aston has incurred no major repair costs or breakdown during its 6+ years ownership, roughly a **third** of the service / MOT cost is made up of small repairs and brake pads highlighted during servicing. These totalled almost £2,000 exactly, spread over the 6 years.

Overall, as the Aston Martin appears then to be costing a **similar amount to own** each year versus the Alfa Romeo but as it's only covering **a third of the miles**, the cost per mile ends up being three times higher. Using the Vauxhall from 30 years ago as a benchmark again, a monthly cost of around £420 is maybe not so bad after all and my combined motoring costs of £767 a month for two cars are not so extreme when compared to the real cost of any of the Personal Contract Purchase deals available on middle-of-the-range, nice cars today. These often cost around £495 a month after including the initial deposit and a true cost of around £750 a month after factoring in petrol, tyres, insurance and servicing. So I'm running two pre-owned top spec cars for the price of one new mid ranged car.

Author's note

*In case you are wondering, if I sold the Alfa and just kept my Aston Martin for circa 10,000 miles per annum of motoring I estimate the cost per mile would drop to **£0.80** (as all the expensive costs like servicing are being amortised over a larger volume) and the total monthly cost would be around £760, so about the same as keeping two cars and splitting the mileage by purpose. Even at this reduced per mile rate it's still almost **double** the amount you can claim back from the tax-man if using your car for business, so beware! Running a business just for the car doesn't stack up financially at all!*

Chapter 18

Misnomers

Before I had even taken delivery of my Aston Martin I had a few pre-conceptions about what the experience would be like. I'd assumed most people would be a bit envious, but in practice not many let it impact their behaviour. I'd assumed no impact from other road users and pedestrians, plainly this was **very wrong, and mostly in an enjoyable way**. I'd assumed out of control running costs and reliability issues whereas in practice it's been a great car for daily use. I had of course also assumed that a nice car is great for the image and helps pull the girls and even though I wasn't in the market for such a thing I can honestly say it's had zero impact on my marketability. It also sadly makes no such impact on my status as a stand-in for 007 in the next film franchise.

Editor's note

I think these things say more about your looks than those of the car!

Author's Note

Cruel but undoubtedly true!

Chapter 19

Whatever Next?

At regular frequency Mrs H (the wife again) says, pardon my language, *but when are you going to sell the bl**dy thing?* and whilst I do consider selling the Aston from time to time, especially after an unusual squeak from somewhere under its skin, a single journey home anywhere on a sunny day is enough to change the mind and remind me I'm glad to own such a lovely creation (the car, not the wife, but she's OK too) – hence how a planned 12/24 month ownership period (the car not the wife) has now crept up soon to be seven years at the time of writing.

I do from time to time consider revisiting the garages selling a portfolio of luxury vehicles and **switching into another luxury brand**, so maybe a Lamborghini, simply because that would be outrageous, a Ferrari, as shouldn't everyone try and own one? Or maybe a more sensible Bentley, but then these seem to be favoured by rappers, which is hardly my style.

Ultimately though I'm yet to be convinced that these cars would be a step up, even if they are more expensive and it's almost guaranteed that young lads would **stop with the thumbs-up** sign and maybe instead graduate to the key-down-the-paintwork sign instead, something that rarely seems to trouble Aston owners.

Maybe that's because they are British, maybe a tad more old-fashioned. But it's a package that's hard to give up when most people are so positive and supportive about it – and I've not been called a yuppie once.

Editor's note

That's because you are too old!

One thing I am considering is setting up a charity with the lucky owners of other luxury cars so we can take disadvantaged, disabled or simply ambitious youngsters for a spin so they get a great experience to remember and something to post on their own goal board if that's their thing!

If you are one of those car owners, please do get in touch via stuart@seriouslyhelpful.co.uk

Chapter 20

Would I recommend buying an Aston Martin?

This is obviously the $64,000 question and not such a different amount from what a luxury car may end up costing you, unless you too go pre-owned! It's therefore a great way to end my book.

I can honestly say that I have **enjoyed almost every day of my journey through the world of motoring with Aston Martin** hence why a planned 12/24 month ownership period has extended now to almost 7 years. It puts a smile on my face every time an imaginary schoolboy waves and does a thumbs up as I drive past, and it's great to know you are hacking-off a fair proportion of oh-look-at-me drivers of Audis, Mercedes, BMW and Porsches – and obviously I apologise profusely if you are one of the rarer nice owners of such marques and have stumbled into this book by mistake!

You may lose a few *friends* along the way but then again if you take advantage of things like joining the Owners' Club, you're sure to make a few new ones too, plus all those new people who make positive comments when you're out and about, even filling up with fuel. So on balance that's a positive thing.

It's also very nice to think you are driving a British car, although how much of the car is really made here is of course open to debate with most car parts manufacturers being global enterprises – Aston themselves claim that **just under half** of the cars' components come from the UK. And once the new Glamorgan factory comes on line it's probably more accurate to say you have an odds on chance to be driving a Welsh car, albeit backed by Kuwaitis and Italians, but the good intentions of buying home-built were still there and deserve applauding!

Editor's note:

Given the low volumes you could have said a Welsh Rarebit?

If I could re-invent myself as an Avatar I'd pick a hybrid of Jamiroquai, Guy Martin, Will Smith and Justin Timberlake.....it would obviously be an odd Avatar to say the least! Ownership of an Aston has brought me zero percent closer to being anything like these idols but at least the first have been, and may still be, Aston fans, alongside an illustrious list of other owners as follows:

Ben Affleck	Michael Jordan	Wayne Rooney
David Beckham	Kerry Katona	Jason Statham
Halle Berry	Queen Latifah	Slash (whoever that is)
Pierce Brosnan & Daniel Craig (Obviously)	Jay Leno (& every other car!)	Steven Spielberg

Prince Charles	Elle Macpherson	Sylvester Stallone
Chris Eubank	Eddie Murphy	Jimmy White (probably won it for a 147 break)
Hugh Grant	Rafael Nadal	**You?**

Can you honestly think of **any** kind of club you could belong to with this list of famous names alongside your own? It adds to the mystique of an Aston Martin and makes you feel just a little bit more special yourself – I can't imagine any other cars doing the same.

It's a pleasant surprise that you can pick up such a smashing and stimulating car for about the same as a top of the range foreign import, even more so that the running costs aren't as horrendous as you might have feared (**not that I can promise** your experience will match mine, but I do believe the modern luxury cars like an Aston are increasingly capable of being used on an everyday basis). The depreciation isn't generally as bad as a normal car and it's even possible to unearth a rare surprise, for example, in the case of my Vantage, as I believe it's one of the original Press cars, hence has a top spec and a slightly more interesting history. This may well add to its value when I eventually come to sell and may help cut my costs overall.

Every Aston Martin has its own file at the factory charting its birth and launch into the world alongside important things like the chassis and engine numbers and I believe in future they may even come with a real life **birth certificate** – that's certainly not something you get with an everyday car, however expensive or gadget laden it may be.

The occasional unusual noise or warning light is of course not great but in my experience these often stop as soon as they start, so provided you are not the kind of car owner that worries over every little thing and dives for the nearest garage, these experiences will be more than rewarded by the sheer joy of driving your Aston – it really does put the smile back on your face after a bad day!

Go on – you know you deserve it!

PS. And if, unlike many others, you go the extra mile to be courteous to other road users and let people out even when it's your right of way, you can do something special by helping in your own small way to improve the reputation for British politeness, and by association, of Aston Martin as a brand and maybe even James Bond himself!

Footnote

James Bond & 007?

We started and finished our journey by talking about James Bond and the 007 cars so why not finish off in style with a bit more information about him that's also food for thought?

Isn't it a pretty general belief that James Bond **always** drives an Aston? In actual fact, ignoring all the plethora of vehicles commandeered in chases or driven by villains, and focusing only on those supposedly **owned** by James himself, then Astons make up only around **30%** of his cars! Who would have guessed that? If I'd known I might have got a BMW or Lincoln!

But it's still nice to feel the association with the films when you drive any Aston Martin and unforgettable when people smile and wave, probably as a result!

Image courtesy Pixabay

© Stuart Haining April 2018

BITE-SIZED BOOKS

Bite-Sized Lifestyle Books are designed to provide insights and ideas about our lives and the pressures on all of us and what we can do to change our environment and ourselves.

They are deliberately short, easy to read, books helping readers to gain a different perspective. They are firmly based on personal experience and where possible successful actions and aren't academic or research-based.

The most successful people all share an ability to focus on what really matters, keeping things simple and understandable. As Stephen Covey famously said, "The main thing is to keep the main thing, the main thing".

But what exactly is the main thing?

Bite-Sized Books were conceived to help answer precisely that question crisply and fast and, of course, be engaging to read, written by people who are experienced and successful in their field.

The brief? Distil the "main things" into a book that can be read by an intelligent non-expert comfortably in around 60 minutes. Make sure the book enables the reader with specific ideas and plenty of examples drawn from real life. In some cases the books are a virtual mentor.

Bite-Sized Books don't cover every eventuality, but they are written from the heart by successful people who are happy to share their experience with you and give you the benefit of their success.

We have avoided jargon – or explained it where we have used it as a shorthand – and made few assumptions about the reader, except that they are literate and numerate, and that they can adapt and use what we suggest to suit their own, individual purposes.

They can be read straight through at one easy sitting and then used as a support while you are thinking further about the issues that most of us face.

Bite-Sized Books Catalogue

Business Books

Paul Davies

Developing a Business Case

Making a Persuasive Argument out of Your Numbers

Paul Davies

Developing a Business Plan

Making a Persuasive Case for Your Business

Paul Davies

Contract Management for Non-Specialists

Paul Davies

Developing Personal Effectiveness in Business

Paul Davies

A More Effective Sales Team

Sales Management Focused on Sales People

Tim Emmett

Bid for Success

Building the Right Strategy and Team

Nigel Greenwood

Why You Should Welcome Customer Complaints

And What to Do About Them

Nigel Greenwood

Six Things that All Customer Want

A Practical Guide to Delivering Simply Brilliant Customer Service

Stuart Haining

> The Practical Digital Marketeer – Volume 1
>
>> Digital Marketing – Is It Worth It and Your First Steps

Stuart Haining

> The Practical Digital Marketeer – Volume 2
>
>> Planning for Success

Stuart Haining

> The Practical Digital Marketeer – Volume 3
>
>> Your Website

Stuart Haining

> The Practical Digital Marketeer – Volume 4
>
>> Be Sociable – Even If You Hate It

Stuart Haining

> The Practical Digital Marketeer – Volume 5
>
>> Your On-going Digital Marketing

Christopher Hosford

> Great Business Meetings! Greater Business Results
>
>> Transforming Boring Time-Wasters into Dynamic Productivity Engines

Ian Hucker

> Risk Management in IT Outsourcing
>
>> 9 Short Steps to Success

Marcus Lopes and Carlos Ponce

> Retail Wars
>
>> May the Mobile be with You

Maiqi Ma

> Win with China

> > Acclimatisation for Mutual Success Doing Business with China

Elena Mihajloska

> Bridging the Virtual Gap

> > Building Unity and Trust in Remote Teams

Rob Morley

> Agile in Business

> > A Guide for Company Leadership

Gillian Perry

> Managing the People Side of Change

> > Ten Short Steps to Success in IT Outsourcing

Saibal Sen

> Next Generation Service Management

> > An Analytics Driven Approach

Don Sharp

> Nothing Happens Until You Sell Something

> > A Personal View of Selling Techniques

Lifestyle Books

Anna Corthout

> Alive Again

> > My Journey to Recovery

Phil Davies

> Don't Worry Be Happy
>> A Personal Journey

Phil Davies

> Feel the Fear and Pack Anyway
>> Around the World in 284 Days

Stuart Haining

> My Other Car is an Aston
>> A Practical Guide to Ownership and Other Excuses to Quit Work and Start a Business

Regina Kerschbaumer

> Yoga Coffee and a Glass of Wine
>> A Yoga Journey

Gillian Perry

> Capturing the Celestial Lights
>> A Practical Guide to Imagining the Northern Lights

Arthur Worrell

> A Grandfather's Story
>> Arthur Worrell's War

Public Affairs Books

Eben Black

> Lies Lunch and Lobbying
>> PR, Public Affairs and Political Engagement – A Guide

Printed in Great Britain
by Amazon